URANUS
Cold and Blue

by Chaya Glaser

Consultant: Karly M. Pitman, PhD
Planetary Science Institute
Tucson, Arizona

BEARPORT
PUBLISHING

New York, New York

Credits
Cover, © NASA; TOC, © NASA; 4–5, © NASA; 6–7, © Wikipedia & NASA; 8, © NASA/JPL; 9, © Andrzej Wojcickl/Science Photo Library; 10, © NASA/SDO (AIA); 11, © NASA; 12–13, © Andrzej Wojcicki/Science Photo Library; 14, © NASA; 15, © NASA/JPL; 16, © NASA; 17, © NASA/JPL; 18, © NASA/JPL; 20–21, © NASA & Wikipedia; 23TL, © Kritchanut/Shutterstock; 23TR, © NASA & Wikipedia; 23BL, © NASA/JPL; 23BR, © Gary Whitton/Shutterstock.

Publisher: Kenn Goin
Senior Editor: Joyce Tavolacci
Creative Director: Spencer Brinker
Design: Debrah Kaiser
Photo Researcher: Michael Win

Library of Congress Cataloging-in-Publication Data

Glaser, Chaya, author.
  Uranus : cold and blue / by Chaya Glaser.
     pages cm. — (Out of this world)
  Includes bibliographical references and index.
  ISBN 978-1-62724-567-8 (library binding) — ISBN 1-62724-567-7 (library binding)
  1. Uranus (Planet)—Juvenile literature. I. Title.
  QB681.G53 2015
  523.47—dc23
                                      2014037336

For more information, write to Bearport Publishing Company, Inc., 45 West 21st Street, Suite 3B, New York, New York 10010. Printed in the United States of America.

10 9 8 7 6 5 4 3 2 1

CONTENTS

What planet is an icy blue ball of gases and liquids?

URANUS!

5

Uranus is part of Earth's Solar System.

JUPITER

MARS

VENUS

EARTH

MERCURY

SUN

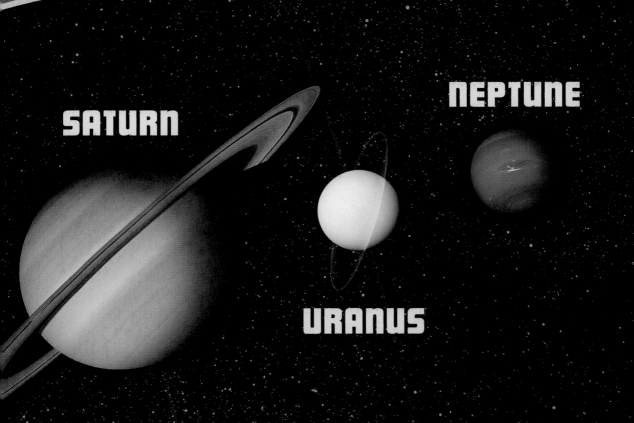

SATURN

URANUS

NEPTUNE

It's the seventh planet from the Sun.

Uranus is much larger than Earth.

Sixty-three Earths could fit inside Uranus.

EARTH

URANUS

9

The planet is super cold and icy.

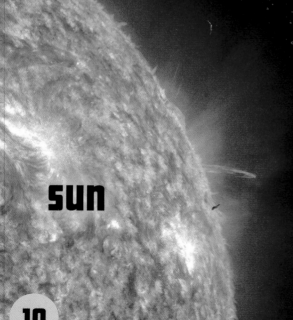

sun

URANUS

Uranus's temperature can dip to about −366°F (−221°C)!

Uranus is mostly made of gases and liquids.

The gases help give the planet its blue color.

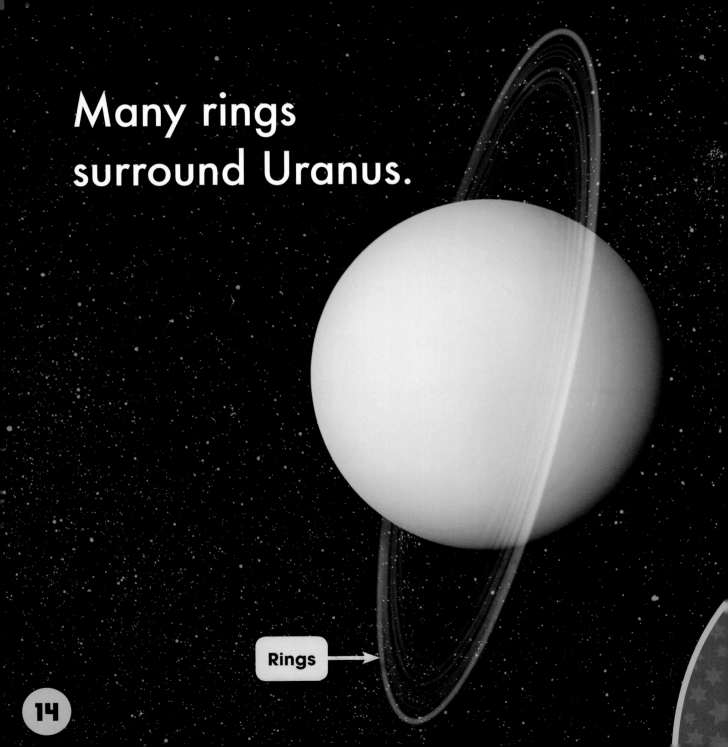

Many rings
surround Uranus.

Rings →

Close-up view of Uranus's rings

These rings are made of dark bits of rock and ice.

Most planets, such as Earth, spin like a top.

Uranus, however, spins on its side.

EARTH

URANUS

Only one spacecraft has flown past Uranus.

It's called *Voyager 2*.

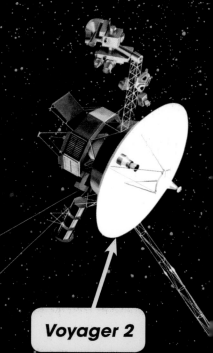

Voyager 2

Voyager 2 took photos of Uranus's five largest moons.

URANUS

It also discovered many new moons!

URANUS VERSUS EARTH

URANUS	VERSUS	EARTH
Seventh planet from the Sun	POSITION	Third planet from the Sun
31,518 miles (50,723 km) across	SIZE	7,918 miles (12,743 km) across
About −357°F (−216°C)	AVERAGE TEMPERATURE	59°F (15°C)
27	NUMBER OF MOONS	One
13	NUMBER OF RINGS	Zero

gases (GASS-iz)   substances that float in the air that are neither liquid nor solid; many gases are invisible

Solar System (SOH-lur SISS-tuhm)   the Sun and everything that circles around it, including the eight planets

spacecraft (SPAYSS-kraft) a vehicle that can travel in space

temperature (TEM-pur-uh-chur)   how hot or cold something is

INDEX

READ MORE

Landau, Elaine. *Uranus (True Books: Space).* New York: Children's Press (2008).

Lawrence, Ellen. *Uranus: The Sideways-Spinning Planet (Zoom Into Space).* New York: Ruby Tuesday Books (2014).

LEARN MORE ONLINE

To learn more about Uranus, visit
www.bearportpublishing.com/OutOfThisWorld

ABOUT THE AUTHOR

Chaya Glaser enjoys looking up at the stars and reading stories about the constellations. When she's not admiring the night sky, she can be found playing musical instruments.